PRAYING LIKE PAUL >>

Learning to Pray
the Kingdom
for Those You Love

PrayerShop
Publishing

Terre Haute, Indiana

Prayer Shop Publishing is the publishing arm of Harvest Prayer Ministries and the Church Prayer Leaders Network. Harvest Prayer Ministries exists to transform lives through teaching prayer.

Its online prayer store, www.prayershop.org, has more than 600 prayer resources available for purchase.

ISBN: 9781935012054

Library of Congress Control Number: 2008911408

1 2 3 4 5 6 7 8 9 10 | 2015 2014 2013 2012 2011 2010 2009 2008

TABLE OF CONTENTS

Part 3: Prayer and the Ministry of the Gospel

Part 4: Praying for Other Believers

INTRODUCTION

A Better Way to Pray

For the past decade, I have been an aficionado of prayer. I am interested in it, study and analyze it, and try to practice it longer and in more powerful ways. But it has not always been that way.

Though I grew up in the church, came to saving faith in Christ as a six-year-old, and had a wonderful Christian upbringing and discipleship, I was not devoted much to prayer until my early thirties. Oh, I knew how to pray, but it was never a part of my daily walk with God. It was never a passion. It wasn't until 1989-90 that I began moving from being a crisis pray-er (able to pray much only if there was something significant in my life to pray about) to having a passion for prayer.

That year, three things happened which caused me to move forward in the area of prayer: I had an experience that many would call a filling of the Holy Spirit; I received an assignment to write a study guide to A.W. Tozer's classic book *The Pursuit of God*; and the responsibility of my new position at Christian Publications, the publishing house I worked for, scared me so much that I needed to pray.

My experience with the Holy Spirit forever changed my relationship with God; something within me was continually drawing me to God, desiring to commune with Him. Working on *The Pursuit of God* increased my hunger for God tenfold. And the fear I had in taking over a department that published books on the deeper spiritual life simply drove me to God in desperation. I hadn't come up through the ranks in publishing. God had just plopped me into the middle of an expanding company through an unusual set of circumstances. Though I had authority, I didn't know what I was doing. I didn't want to make mistakes in selecting books.

But even though I was growing in my prayer life—I was praying each day, I was pouring my heart out to God and connecting with Him—I would certainly not say I was a "good" pray-er. When it came to praying for anything other than my own situations, I was weak. I tried to intercede for friends and family, but struggled. I valiantly tried keeping lists and praying for what I had been asked to pray for. But it was dull and lifeless. Why? Because I was praying the only way I knew how, based on what I had seen growing up in church.

For much of my life I attended prayer meetings, where I, like everyone there, would dutifully remember all those who gave requests. Often I would write out a list and stick it in my Bible—where it would stay (along with other collected prayer lists for other prayer meetings) until my quarterly old-bulletin prayer-list cleaning, when I would throw it (them) away. Usually the things on these lists were very uninspiring—someone's third cousin who was laid off from work; another's kid who had a math test the next day; maybe a missionary or two whom the church supported. There was nothing there I could pray passionately about. If I ever prayed for something from that prayer meeting list during the week, all I ever prayed was for the obvious, what I specifically had been asked to pray. Passion only came when I really cared about what (or whom) I was praying for.

The Change

In December of 1994, I married JoLyn, a single mom, who had an eight-year-old daughter, Amy. Suddenly I had two more people in my life, whom I loved, who were very important to me. They easily became a part of my regular prayer life. But over the years, as I have prayed for them, I noticed something: I have sustained a greater level of prayer for them—in length of time, but also in intensity and passion—when I have prayed for character qualities, rather than when I prayed for a specific, concrete thing.

I did pray for specific things—school issues with Amy, new friends for Jo, who had been uprooted from her life in Pennsylvania. But it was my praying for character qualities that filled me with passion and, I believe, made the most difference in their lives. And let me be clear: I was not praying for character traits because I thought they were seriously lacking in their lives, but because I felt God leading me to do so.

For my wife, I started regularly praying for joy. It wasn't that she was depressed. I just knew that she had gone through incredible pain in the circumstances surrounding the ending of her first marriage. I just had a sense that she needed to experience a deeper level of joy. For Amy, I prayed that God would develop her wonderful sensitive spirit. He had an ultimate purpose for it; I wanted to see it fully used by Him. A few years later, when Amy felt a call to be a missionary, I started praying in a new vein. I pictured her as a strong woman of God. What would she need to be used of God on the mission field? I began to pray—and still do—for those characteristics as they come to mind.

A few years later, I became an elder and a prayer leader at my church. There, instead of focusing my prayers back on those everyday needs, I began trying to pray bigger things for the people under my care. I wanted to see God do great things in the life of our church and the lives of our people. Transforming things! Instead of focusing prayers on the everyday "God, please let their life be normal again" prayers we usually voice, I tried to pray prayers that sought God's purposes for their lives. Prayers that asked God to bring glory to His Son through these situations and lives.

I began being struck more and more by the prayers of Paul (which we'll look at in the remainder of this book). Paul had people with huge problems under his care, people who were facing life-and-death situations. Yet in all his recorded prayers, nowhere do I see that he prayed for specific answers to everyday situations. (Yes, he prayed for himself, that his "thorn in the flesh" would be removed. But remember, God said "no," so he stopped praying about that.) Don't get me wrong. I would be surprised if Paul didn't pray for some specific things for people he knew, so I am not saying that we should never pray for specific answers. But, since all of Paul's recorded prayers were in a different vein, I wonder if a majority of our prayers for ourselves and people shouldn't be of the same kind.

Most of us pray for those little answerables for each other. Sometimes we see some answers, but most of the time not. Over time, many stop praying because they do not see enough things answered. Often they even fail to see God move in a situation because they are so focused on what they *want* to see happen. We keep trying to bolster faith and claim those promises in Scripture which tell us we can ask for anything and it will happen. But often, more and more, our prayers resemble fate rather than faith, and "hope so" rather than belief.

Our weak, "I hope God will do this" prayers take their toll. Most of us have tepid prayer lives. We don't get excited about praying with others. Our churches' corporate prayer experiences are anemic and dull. And yet God says that He wants to do immeasurably more than we can ask or think (Ephesians 3:20). Most don't think to even ask—and if we do ask, we only ask for the little answerables: "make my life normal again."

A few years ago, a pastor friend—we'll call him Bill—revealed something very interesting about his ministry; something that I think is equally true in churches all across the Western world. Even though at the time, on the outside, he had a nice, stable—and to most eyes—effective ministry, he told me something shocking. He said that in his fifteen-plus years of ministry, he could only point to one person who was a believer when he first came into Bill's church (not counting people who came to Christ in his ministry) who clearly grew in his relationship with God while under Bill's ministry. He meant that over a period of time, the evidence showed that this person clearly went deeper in his walk with God; it was obvious. Bill is not alone. Many churches do not see spiritual growth in their people. People may gain spiritual knowledge but don't really grow deeper spiritually. (Whatever level of spiritual depth they are on when they join a church is the same level they are on years later.)

Like Bill, that realization should radically change both the way we do discipleship and, more importantly, the way we pray for fellow believers. We need to pray more for spiritual development and less for comfort and ease. We need to pray more for the Holy Spirit to transform and less for things that make the lives of those we love normal. That's radical.

Well, this book is about radically changing the way you pray! I believe Paul has some solid ideas on how and what to pray for those we love. We're going to look at those ideas and allow them to shape the way we pray—for ourselves and for others.

Instead of seeking God for the little answerables, you're going to learn to seek Him for eternal things: God's glory, kingdom expansion, and God's will. May your prayer life—and the spiritual lives of those for whom you are praying—never be the same!

BEFORE YOU START

∞

What Did Paul Know?

In his second epistle to the Corinthians, the apostle Paul said some interesting things about prayer. He began the book by reminding the Corinthian believers that they shared in his sufferings. Then he filled them in a little on the ways he had suffered in his latest missionary journey:

> We do not want you to be uninformed, brothers, about the hardships we suffered in the province of Asia. We were under great pressure, far beyond our ability to endure, so that we despaired even of life. Indeed, in our hearts we felt the sentence of death. But this happened that we might not rely on ourselves but on God, who raises the dead. He has delivered us from such a deadly

peril, and he will deliver us. On him we have set our hope that he will continue to deliver us, as you help us by your prayers. Then many will give thanks on our behalf for the gracious favor granted us in answer to the prayers of many. (2 Corinthians 1:8-11)

This was not a missionary writing his supporters, saying how blessed he was knowing that people back home were praying. No, Paul knew that prayer truly affected the kingdom; that prayer brought results; that prayer did something in the heavenlies that moved the hand of God and beat back the kingdom of darkness's attempt to thwart his ministry. He recognized that they were literally joining his journey through their prayers. Without them, Paul would not have made it!

The Essential Aspect

Prayer is *the most vital aspect* of a believer's walk with God. Bible reading and memorization are extremely important for our spiritual health and growth. But there are many believers around the world who do not have a Bible, and while significantly hampered, they can still grow. Fellowshipping with other believers in community is certainly necessary for our spiritual life. But there are believers who cannot participate in meaningful fellowship, and they still grow. Listening to preaching and teaching can stimulate us to go deeper in our faith. But again, many believers do not have the wealth of teachers we in the West have, but they still mature in their faith. Without prayer, however, real growth does not occur much.

In a given church, there are believers who are growing deeper in their faith and those who are not. In most churches the ratio of growing believers to nongrowing ones is probably one out of five or worse. The difference? Those who are growing probably have a prayer life, or at least are working to develop one. Or another possibility: they have someone who is significantly praying for their spiritual growth.

And that's what Paul knew. He realized the importance of praying key spiritual growth principles into people's lives. Paul was concerned about lots of people all across Asia Minor (modern Turkey) and throughout Greece and Rome. Despite the great physical and material needs these folks must have had, Paul didn't seem to focus on those things in his prayers for them. Instead, Paul focused on spiritual health in these believers. Their growth in wisdom and understanding, revelation, and love dominated his prayers for them.

Paul also did something that I find very intriguing. He practiced what I call "praying the process." That is, he seemed to pray more for the process of growth in people's lives than the end result. In most of Paul's prayers recorded in the epistles, we see two little words near the middle: "so that." Paul prayed something *so that* something else would happen. For example, look at these two prayers:

This is my prayer: that your love may abound more and more in knowledge and depth of insight, so that you may be able to discern what is best and may be pure and blameless until the day of Christ, filled with the fruit of righteousness that comes through Jesus Christ—to the glory and praise of God. (Philippians 1:9-11)

I pray that you may be active in sharing your faith, so

> that you will have a full understanding of every good
> thing we have in Christ. (Philemon 6)

He had some results in mind (be more discerning, live pure and blameless lives, understand who we are in Christ), but he focused more on praying the path toward those things (love, active in sharing what God was doing in one's life). He prayed the process, not the results.

I am sure in some of Paul's nonrecorded prayers, he prayed for specific things, but in the ones God chose to record, he prayed for spiritual development. What should that say to us? Not that we should never pray for specific results, but maybe that a significant part of our prayer agenda—for ourselves and those we love—should focus on spiritual growth.

So what's in it for me? you may wonder.

We need to learn to pray the themes Paul prayed—both for ourselves and others. That's what *Praying Like Paul* is all about—learning to focus prayer on spiritual things rather than earthly concerns. Learning to pray more for spiritual growth and health in the lives of people than for their lives to be normal and problem free. Focusing less on the "little answerables" and more on the "kingdom getting glory results."

How to Use This Book

Praying Like Paul appears to be set up like a devotional. It can be used that way. Read one chapter each day and focus on the Scripture passage of the day. Then pray whatever that day's theme focuses on. You will certainly get something out of that, and it can influence how you pray. I suggest you use it differently, however.

My suggestion: read it all the way through—in one sitting if possible. It won't take more than a few hours. You will also need your Bible, as most chapters' prayers are put in the context of surrounding verses, which you are asked to read. As you read, see what's there, what subjects Paul focuses his prayer on. But I also suggest that you read it a little differently than you might read a normal book.

Before you read, start with prayer. Ask the Holy Spirit to do three things:

- Ask Him to use this resource to improve the effectiveness of your prayers.
- Ask the Holy Spirit to reveal some specific spiritual qualities He wants to grow in you.
- Ask Him to connect in your mind the qualities in the Scripture passage with loved ones for whom you are praying.

After praying this, if the Holy Spirit brings to mind a person for whom the content of a particular chapter would be good to pray, jot his or her name on the page. (Put your own name down if the Holy Spirit pricks you that it would be good to pray this for yourself.) Don't do more than that during the first reading.

After completing the book, go back and look at the pages where you wrote down a name. Don't be alarmed if there are only a couple. Next—whether in the same sitting, or a day or so later—spend some time rereading those chapters. Ask the Holy Spirit to shape what you should pray for the person.

Finally, go to prayer for that person. I recommend that you begin by writing a simple prayer to pray. But you can also go to prayer, and at a point in your prayers where you feel released to do so, write out the prayer. This can give you a stimulus for further prayer as you come back to the chapter in the future.

This entire process of asking the Holy Spirit to bring to mind people for whom He wants you to pray Paul's spiritual themes can be done again and again. Do it whenever you feel a release from the current prayers you are praying. Maybe God has a new prayer assignment for you.

My ultimate goal with this book, however, is to get "praying the process" to become a habit in your ongoing prayer life. I hope and pray that you will soon begin to think twice before just praying the obvious results in a person's situation. Instead, you will think, *What spiritual fruit might the Father want to grow in* _____ *as he or she goes through this situation? Lord, what would you have me pray for* _____ *?*

Lord, change our prayer lives forever as we study this book. Help us to refocus our prayers for people on Your eternal, kingdom-growing agenda. Amen.

Part 1

KNOWING AND PRAISING GOD

Our Glorious Inheritance

Ephesians 1:17-18
Read Ephesians 1

Many believers never grasp the depth of relationship that is possible with Jesus Christ. They come to faith—at least they believe in Jesus as the Christ, as their Savior—but they never grow to the point of a vibrant relationship with Him.

Paul knew that the Ephesians believers—like yourself and those you love—could go so much deeper in their walk with God. Paul described such a walk as "the glorious inheritance in the saints," and it is fueled by Christ's "incomparably great power." Let his prayer be a model for you in seeking that kind of a spiritual walk for yourself and those you love.

> **I keep asking that the God of our Lord Jesus Christ, the glorious Father, may give you the Spirit of wisdom and revelation, so that you may know him better. I pray also that the eyes of your heart may be enlightened in order that you may know the hope to which he has called you, the riches of his glorious inheritance in the saints, and his incomparably great power for us who believe. (Ephesians 1:17–18)**

What did Paul pray for? He asked for a spirit of wisdom and revelation and that the Ephesians' hearts would be open. Why did he pray for those things? So they would know Jesus better and they would have His hope and power.

Wisdom signifies both knowledge—knowing things, facts—and good judgment. It is learning more about God and having the discernment to process all that you know of God into Christlike living. Revelation can mean understanding or an ability to hear from God. But praying for "*a spirit* of wisdom and revelation" implies so much more. To me it is asking for an attitude of seeking the things of God—and God Himself. Yes, Paul wanted knowledge for the Ephesians, but with a passionate heart as well. "Open the eyes of their hearts," he prayed. That goes beyond simply believing in something with our heads. That is an ability to see into another dimension with faith and understanding. And that's an important aspect of a vibrant Christian life.

Many believers struggle to move head knowledge into the heart . . . into day-to-day living out of one's faith through the power of

God. That is our inheritance on earth—the ability to let the power of Christ flow through us, living His life through us.

Let this thought be a starting point for your prayers—for yourself and those whom you love.

Prayer

Gracious Father, I ask You to give _____ a much stronger spirit of wisdom and revelation. Reveal Yourself to him (or her) in greater and greater ways. Let _____ develop an ability to see things as You see them—with spiritual eyes. Father, reveal Jesus to him. Give _____ a sense of the hope he has in You, of the riches he has as Your child. May _____ understand and utilize the power You have made available to him. I pray this in the mighty name of Jesus, my Lord. Amen.

My prayer for: _____

_____

_____

_____

_____

_____

_____

_____

_____

_____

The Immeasurably More

Ephesians 3:16-21
Read Ephesians 3

When we, as believers contemplate who Jesus Christ is, our pictures of Him vary. While we all recognize what He did on the cross—saving us from our sins, giving us new life and access to the throne room of God—many of us don't understand who we are in Christ.

Some view Him as a friend. Some as Almighty God. Some as our Provider. Few of us have a complete picture of Him. That comes through spiritual growth. The more years we are believers (if we desire to go deeper), the more we understand. The more we understand, the easier it is to walk a Spirit-empowered life.

Paul knew the mystery of Christ. And he was trying to help the Ephesian believers understand everything they had in their relationship with Christ. As he explained the mystery of Christ, he shared a prayer he was praying for them:

> I pray that out of his glorious riches he may strengthen you with power through his Spirit in your inner being, so that Christ may dwell in your hearts through faith. And I pray that you, being rooted and established in love, may have power, together with all the saints, to grasp how wide and long and high and deep is the love

of Christ, and to know this love that surpasses knowl-edge—that you may be filled to the measure of all the fullness of God.

Now to him who is able to do immeasurably more than all we ask or imagine, according to his power that is at work within us, to him be glory in the church and in Christ Jesus throughout all generations, for ever and ever! Amen. (Ephesians 3:16-21)

Paul prayed for inner strength and power so that faith might grow in them. He prayed for an outpouring of the depths of God's love, so that they might realize the fullness of Christ within them, so that they would walk in all the power of God. He closed with a benediction—a declaration—that the God who always does more than we think He will do—that God will bring glory to His Son, Jesus, in and through them.

Now that's a prayer I want people praying for me. I want to understand the fullness of Christ in my life; I want to understand the depths of Christ's love working in and through me. And I want that for others. When was the last time that you prayed for a friend or family member to be filled to the measure of all the fullness of Christ? I wonder what that would do in one's life if that happened!

∾

Prayer

Father, I pray that You would give _____ strength and power in her (or his) spirit, a strength and power that will grow her faith in You to completely new levels. Take her deeper into Your mysteries. Let her get a greater sense and understanding of Your love for her, of Your love for Your body, the church. I pray that through that deeper love, _____ would be filled to the full measure of everything You are and have for her. Display Your power in _____'s life by doing a greater work than anyone can imagine or comprehend. May the evidence of You in_____'s life be so strong that everyone would point to the fact that only You could do such a work! I pray this in the mighty name of Jesus, Amen.

My prayer for: _____

_____

_____

_____

_____

_____

_____

_____

Praying to Know God's Will

Colossians 1:9-14
Read Colossians 1:9-14

"How to Know God's Will!" That was a popular topic in my youth. I remember going to a number of seminars on that subject at teen conferences I attended. Books were written on it. I'm sure I got something out of the seminars, but I remember continuing to struggle with that concept.

I wanted to make right decisions in line with God's will. But I never really felt confident that I was doing so. I do know (both from experience and from hearing it in those seminars long past) that there seems to be a connection between spending time with God, gaining a knowledge of Him—who He was, what He was about—and having confidence in knowing God's will.

Each one of us wants to know God's will—both for ourselves and for the others we love and pray for. Paul wanted that for the believers in Colosse. That's what he prayed in Colossians 1:9-14:

> For this reason, since the day we heard about you, we have not stopped praying for you and asking God to fill you with the knowledge of his will through all spiritual wisdom and understanding. And we pray this in order that you may live a life worthy of the Lord and may please him in every way: bearing fruit in every good work, growing in the knowledge of God, being

strengthened with all power according to his glorious might so that you may have great endurance and patience, and joyfully giving thanks to the Father, who has qualified you to share in the inheritance of the saints in the kingdom of light. For he has rescued us from the dominion of darkness and brought us into the kingdom of the Son he loves, in whom we have redemption, the forgiveness of sins.

It must be that finding God's will was tough even in the early church. Paul prayed daily for it. (I certainly can't say I pray for it that much!) Paul added that he prayed for "all spiritual wisdom and understanding." The implication was that knowledge of God's will comes through gaining more insight into spiritual things. And the more we gain an understanding of God, the more we will live out all the will of God that is revealed in Scripture. Hmm, maybe those seminars were right. Instead of worrying about God's will in making this decision or that situation, and only praying for it then, perhaps it should be a daily item on our prayer list. Ultimately, gaining that knowledge will be less for day-to-day decision making and more for day-to-day kingdom living. Why do I say that?

Look at Paul's purpose for praying for knowledge of God's will. He wanted the Colossian believers to live a life worthy of God, bear fruit, and have power, endurance, and strength. He wanted them to be kingdom Christians! Knowledge of God's will was more for living a life that glorified God than for discerning every decision we need to make in life (though choosing what God would want us to choose is certainly important). I believe the more we pray for spiritual wisdom and understanding and a knowledge of God's will, and live out a Spirit-filled life, the "decisions" will become easier and easier. As we live lives that bear fruit, that please God, choosing wisely in the day-to-day decisions will come more naturally.

∞

Prayer

Father, I lift up _____ to You. I pray that You would work mightily in his (or her) life and bless him with spiritual wisdom. Help _____ to desire Your will above his own. Empower _____ with Your Spirit so that he will bear more fruit, will walk worthy of You, and will display patience and endurance. I pray that _____'s life will reflect Your glory to those around him. Encourage him with a greater knowledge of who You are and what You have done for him. Bless _____ with a thankful heart as he lives out his life on a day-to-day basis. Amen.

My prayer for: _____

_____

_____

_____

_____

_____

_____

_____

_____

_____

_____

Overflowing in Praise

1 Timothy 1:17

Read 1 Timothy 1:12-17

Many years ago I had a pastor who seemed to go a little overboard about theological "correctness." Since I was active in worship at the church, several times he and I came into conflict over song choices. It seems he did not want us to sing one of the then-new praise songs, "Bring Forth the Royal Robe," because it was theologically incorrect.

His beef with this song was the line: "Let's give unto the Lord power and strength." "We can't give power and strength to God," was his point. He thought people would think we were giving God something we had that He needed. The song actually was saying, "We ascribe to You, we recognize that You have power and strength." It was similar to the song in Revelation that uses the phrase "be to our God" (Revelation 7:12). The heavenly hosts aren't saying we give to God from our supply of honor, thanks, wisdom, power, strength, etc., but that He has those things in great abundance, and we recognize it and worship Him for it. Maybe the songwriter should have selected a different word, but singing that song was only providing people a verbiage with which to praise God.

Praise is so important to an effective prayer life. In Paul's experience we see praise opening the way of victory as he and Silas sat in prison (Acts 16). Praise affects both the one giving praise and the One receiving praise. Psalm 22 tells us that God inhabits or indwells the praises of His people (22:3, KJV). While we benefit greatly from our praise of God, always remember that we should not praise Him just for the purpose of getting something in mind. We praise Him simply because He is worthy of praise.

After reminding Timothy where Paul had come from and what Christ had done for him (Paul), he launched into verse 17:

Now to the King eternal, immortal, invisible, the only God, be honor and glory for ever and ever. Amen. (1 Timothy 1:17)

His praise spilled over from a heart of gratitude. We need to continually foster the same posture in our lives. When we pray, we often should reminisce about all that God has done for us . . . then let that gratitude overflow into bursts of praise!

Prayer

God, I praise You for who You are. You are so far above us. The King of the universe. The only One worthy of praise and honor. You are worthy of all my praise, for You have all power and strength and honor and wealth; Your glory overshadows all. Lord Jesus, You are the King of all kings, the Lord of all lords, the Ruler who reigns over all. I am humbled in Your presence. Amen.

My prayer for: _____

_____

_____

_____

_____

_____

_____

_____

_____

An Ever-Increasing Glory

1 Thessalonians 5:23

Read 1 Thessalonians 5:12-24

Growing up in the denomination I did, I often heard a big theological word: *sanctification*. It was one of the main emphases of our church. I heard it a lot but didn't know what it meant. To put it simply, sanctification is the process of becoming like Christ.

When we become believers and ask Christ to take control of our lives, the Father wants to do more than forgive our sins and put us on the path to heaven. He wants to shape us into the image of Jesus. Paul put it this way:

> **And we, who with unveiled faces all reflect the Lord's glory, are being transformed into his likeness with ever-increasing glory, which comes from the Lord, who is the Spirit. (2 Corinthians 3:18)**

That's sanctification. Jesus wants to change us into His image. Believers who grow deeper in their faith understand that. The Christian life is one of constant change, constant refining, constant reshaping. Every experience that comes into our lives has a refining purpose, an "ever-increasing glory" purpose. We join the process to an even greater degree if, through prayer, we surrender and open ourselves up to it.

Paul prayed for an increase in this sanctification process in the believers at Thessalonica:

> **May God himself, the God of peace, sanctify you through and through. May your whole spirit, soul and body be kept blameless at the coming of our Lord Jesus Christ. (1 Thessalonians 5:23)**

As we are sanctified, our lives—spirit, soul, and body—reflect that blamelessness Paul also prayed for. Are you praying for the sanctification process in your own life? In the lives of others? That's really what this entire book is about—letting God shape us and refine us into the image of His Son, Jesus.

Prayer

Father, I know You want to transform me into the image of Jesus. I want that in my life. I surrender to Your work in me. Please sanctify those areas of my life that continue to need refining. I want to be kept blameless until the coming of Your Son. Even if it is painful, Father, keep drawing me into a greater walk with You, into a deeper faith and experience of Your Son. In Jesus' name, Amen.

My prayer for: _____

_____

_____

_____

Knowing and Praising God

_____

_____

_____

_____

_____

Part 2

SPIRITUAL GROWTH THROUGH SUFFERING

Overflowing with Hope

Romans 15:13
Read Romans 15:8-16

R ome in the apostle Paul's day was not a good place to be a Christian. In fact, it was a crime to worship anyone or anything but Caesar. Believers there likely experienced intense struggles. They had to live out their faith amid pain, rejection, and even fear for their lives.

Today, Western believers don't face many of those hardships. But our lives are not without pain. We face loss of loved ones due to sickness; we face growing disdain from nonbelievers in our society; we face financial setbacks, loss of jobs, and bad things happening to our kids. All of these things are common in believer's lives.

So Paul's prayer for the Roman believers has implications for us:

May the God of hope fill you with all joy and peace as you trust in him, so that you may overflow with hope by the power of the Holy Spirit. (Romans 15:13)

What did Paul pray for? Joy and peace. Why did he pray for those things? So the believers would overflow with hope.

When you look at the context of the passage around this prayer, another distinction is added. The other verses are all about the gospel going to the Gentiles (non-Jews) and about evangelism. Seeing people—Romans—come to faith in Jesus Christ. So why did Paul, in the middle of a passage on evangelism, pray for joy, peace and hope in the believers?

People who have hope in tough times are very attractive to other people. You know that to be true. Anytime you find a person who is going through something difficult—an illness, pain with a wayward child, or any painful circumstance of life—but doing it with a buoyant spirit, with a smile in his heart, people are drawn to him. Such a person can then share the power of Christ in his life with others. That's what Paul was praying, for Romans believers to rise above their circumstances and let the joy and peace of God shine through their lives. Because people would be attracted to the gospel!

Unfortunately, many modern Western believers have the attitude that life needs to be perfect, or that God promises us a happy life. So any time calamity comes to us or those we care about, we immediately pray, "Lord, remove this. . . . Fix this." But He might want to do something for His kingdom through it. Perhaps as unbelievers watch a Christian go through a trial with great grace, they will come into the kingdom.

So the next time you pray about a difficult situation in someone's life, maybe God would have you pray like Paul. Pray for joy and peace, for hope to fill the believer amidst the difficulty, so that in his overflow of hope, people would be attracted to Christ.

Prayer

Lord Jesus Christ, as _____ walks through this difficult circumstance, would you fill her (or him) with Your peace? Give her joy, despite her pain. Let her eyes be fixed on You. Help her to trust in You—in Your strength, in Your comfort, in Your sovereignty. As she looks to You, may her life overflow with Your hope, and may that attract her friends, family, and coworkers to Jesus Christ. Give her open doors to share her faith and what You are doing in her. Amen.

My prayer for: _____

_____

_____

_____

_____

_____

_____

_____

_____

Praying When You Have Failed

2 Corinthians 13:7-10
Read 2 Corinthians 13

Have you ever felt like a failure when it comes to parenting or discipling others? How do you feel when you pour a part of your life into a child or a person in your small group and she doesn't appear to be thriving spiritually? In fact, she seems to be struggling instead?

I have had that situation several times in my life—both with a child and with spiritual disciples. There is a helplessness that comes. You want the best for that person and think you know what it is, but she is not choosing what you think is best. It can be gut-wrenching, especially if it is a child.

That was what Paul was feeling. He had poured his life into the Corinthian believers. There was much to be thankful for, but as he closed his second letter to them, his frustration came out. He commented on some of the struggles they were having—they seemed to be overly critical of Paul. He felt like a failure in his ministry among them. But when he prayed for them, he tried to rise above his own hurt feelings to focus on what they needed:

> **Now we pray to God that you will not do anything wrong. Not that people will see that we have stood the test but that you will do what is right even though we may seem to have failed. For we cannot do anything against the**

truth, but only for the truth. We are glad whenever we are weak but you are strong; and our prayer is for your perfection. (2 Corinthians 13:7-10)

Are you frustrated by the spiritual life—or lack thereof—in someone (a fellow believer who should know better) you are close to? Rise above that and pray fervently for that individual. Pray that the truth he or she knows deep down would rise to the surface. Pray that the Holy Spirit would bring light, and that it would shine over the darkness Satan is currently bringing to cloud your friend's way. Believe that God can break through in his or her heart!

Prayer

Lord Jesus, You are the Way, the Truth, and the Life. You are the Bringer of light. I bring _____ right now before Your throne. I ask that You would do a work of Truth-bringing to his (or her) heart right now. He is struggling and cannot see the light; he is not making decisions based on Your truth, based on truth he has known and believed in the past. Holy Spirit, shine light in _____'s heart. Give him the courage both to seek Your truth and to walk in it. I pray this in the mighty name of Jesus, Amen.

My prayer for: _____

_____

_____

_____

_____

_____

_____

_____

_____

Peace That Transcends

Have you ever experienced a computer crash? You turn on the computer and it loads and loads and loads, but nothing happens. Or your screen goes blank or locks up, and you can't do anything. I recently experienced that twice in one month. Files lost, e-mails with important information gone. The fear that all the records of our ministry were gone came over me. Can you say, "panic attack"?

We all have situations in our lives that rob us of peace, that work against the joy we try to walk in as believers. But even in the midst of those situations, Paul tells us that we can have the peace of God. In fact, we can have it so strongly that it defies understanding and logic.

Paul wrote to the Philippian believers:

> **Do not be anxious about anything, but in everything, by prayer and petition, with thanksgiving, present your requests to God. And the peace of God, which transcends all understanding, will guard your hearts and your minds in Christ Jesus. (Philippians 4:6-7)**

What Paul was expressing was that when we can pray in the midst of any circumstances, and when we can even have hearts of thanksgiving and praise in the midst of those circumstances, something unusual and supernatural happens. A sense of peace will come from outside ourselves and will provide what we need to walk through the difficult situation. It is literally the peace of God. What does it do? It guards our hearts and minds to keep remembering the truth of God's faithfulness, provision, and love. We do not believe the lies that Satan wants to plant in us: "God doesn't love you or you wouldn't be going through this" or "Give up!" Praying and praising takes us above our circumstances. It gives us the ability to walk out the truth of the next verse:

> **Finally, brothers, whatever is true, whatever is noble, whatever is right, whatever is pure, whatever is lovely, whatever is admirable—if anything is excellent or praiseworthy—think about such things. Whatever you have learned or received or heard from me, or seen in me—put it into practice. And the God of peace will be with you. (4:8-9)** *Surrender + Trust,*

Do you need peace today? What about someone you know? Pray. Ask for peace. Praise God for His attributes—especially those aspects of God's character that you need right now.

Prayer

Father, I thank You that You promised Your peace to us, a peace that is way beyond anything I can muster up. Father, I thank You and praise You for Your goodness, Your faithfulness. I claim right now that peace You promised in Your Word, that peace that transcends knowledge and understanding. I appropriate that ability to think on truthful things, things that are good, lovely, admirable, and praiseworthy. Bless You, Father. You are worthy to be praised! Amen.

My prayer for: _____

ISA 55:11   Joshua 1:8   Mt 6:33
Prov 3:5-6   Ps 32:8   1 Pe 5:7
1 Thes 5:18   Rom 12:1

Memorize Scripture - Can lead
me in times of concern & need.
Cast cares on Christ - once for
all.
Once issue settled no more
anxiety or concern.
Peace - Trust God to handle
situation. God knows all I don't!
Jesus speaks of happens - I can
turn over to Him - Know He
will prove Himself faithful. He
Sensitive to what God wants me to do!
Why kick goads -
Know when God is calling us to
talk with Him - fellowship -
Call to obedience 41

A Life Well Lived

2 Thessalonians 1:11-12
Read 2 Thessalonians 1

Have you ever known fellow believers who had to endure significant hardship, but did it with incredible grace and faith? What did their journey say to those around them? Did people feel drawn to these believers or were the people confused, wondering how the believers could act like they did?

My experience is that most people who endure hardship with grace are very attractive to others. People seem to rally around them more than those who grumble and complain about their situations. A young woman named Angie was in our small group a number of years ago. She suffers with one of those debilitating chronic illnesses that doctors can't seem to figure out. She had been a star athlete in high school and started getting tired, worn out—you know the rest. Now, fifteen years later, she is a young mother struggling to have the energy to take care of her family.

I never have heard a disparaging word from Angie—quite the opposite. I asked her one time if she struggled with the fact that God wasn't healing her. Her answer blessed me. She basically said she would not change anything about her situation. The days she could barely get out of bed were in many ways the sweetest. God met her there with His presence and grace. She had a spiritual depth that many other women her age lack.

The believers in Thessalonica were struggling big time. Persecu-

42

tion and hardship were the norm. But Paul commended them for how they were living out their faith in the midst of these hardships. In the first ten verses of 2 Thessalonians, he wrote that their faith and actions were a model for others to follow. Then he told them how he prayed for them in their situation:

> **With this in mind, we constantly pray for you, that our God may count you worthy of his calling, and that by his power he may fulfill every good purpose of yours and every act prompted by your faith. We pray this so that the name of our Lord Jesus may be glorified in you, and you in him, according to the grace of our God and the Lord Jesus Christ. (2 Thessalonians 1:11–12)**

Notice that Paul did not pray for the hardship to cease. That is hard for us Westerners to grapple with. Somehow, many of our fellow believers (perhaps you included) have come to think that we should have a pain-free life. At least that appears to be the case when we hear people pray. Our thoughts are always to remove the pain and fix the situation.

Paul prayed that God would count the Thessalonians worthy, that He would fulfill every purpose He had for them and every act of faith they attempted. Why did he pray those things? So that the name of Jesus Christ would be given glory! Paul knew that ultimately God would receive more honor, fame, and glory from His people showing grace in the midst of hardship than by removing the hardship.

It is a hard thing to pray for someone going through a tough time. Our love for that person and our human sensibilities say: "Pray that it stops!" But in many situations, perhaps we need to rethink how we should pray.

Prayer

Father, I lift up _____ to You right now. I know it cannot be easy for _____ to be going through the struggles she (or he) is currently experiencing. I take comfort in the fact that You know that more than I do, and You care for and love her. I know, too, that You have purposes for _____ in this situation. Your Word says that everything works together for good to those who love you. You also say that You turn everything Satan intends for harm into a victory. I am asking right now for that victorious power for _____. Fill her with Your grace, mercy, and faith. Work a miracle in her situation, a miracle that will bring glory to Your Son, Jesus. May _____'s life be a testimony of grace to those around her, drawing those observing her life into Your kingdom as a result. I pray this in Jesus' mighty name, Amen.

My prayer for: _____

_____

_____

_____

_____

_____

_____

_____

_____

_____

The Power of Love

Philippians 1:9-11

Read Philippians 1:3-21

When difficult things happen to those we love, our concern and empathy for the pain they are going through often causes us to lose perspective on how we should pray. Because of our love for them, we immediately want to pray them out of the situation. Yet God might be using the situation for a good purpose to be fulfilled in their lives.

That was the situation with Paul. He was imprisoned in Rome. Apparently many were praying for his release. I certainly would have. But Paul told the believers that his being in chains was God's will. It was having a greater impact for the kingdom than if he weren't in chains. He asked the Philippian believers not to worry about his condition. He even told them not to worry about those who were stirring up trouble for him while he could not defend himself.

In the midst of his comments, he told them what he was praying for them—love.

And this is my prayer: that your love may abound more and more in knowledge and depth of insight, so that you may be able to discern what is best and may be pure and blameless until the day of Christ, filled with the fruit of righteousness that comes through Jesus Christ—to the

glory and praise of God. (Philippians 1:9-11)

Love is an amazing force! God is love! Paul was praying for love so that they would grow in their discernment of what was best (God's will and purposes) and that they would live pure and blameless lives. How can an increase of love bring about all that—a deeper recognition of God's purposes and a great desire and ability to live a life pleasing to Him? What would an increase of love in everyone do in your church? What would a deeper level of love do in your marriage and family?

> **Love is patient, love is kind. It does not envy, it does not boast, it is not proud. It is not rude, it is not self-seeking, it is not easily angered, it keeps no record of wrongs. Love does not delight in evil but rejoices with the truth. It always protects, always trusts, always hopes, always perseveres. (1 Corinthians 13:4-7)**

Peter wrote, "Above all, love each other deeply, because love covers over a multitude of sins" (1 Peter 4:8).

Praying for love for yourself and others will have a profound effect on you or those you pray for—on how you view life, on how you handle circumstances, on how you pray for others.

Prayer

Father God, I thank You for Your great love for us. Thank You for the love that sent You to this earth to suffer and die to pay the penalty for our sins. Lord, I want to experience a deeper level of love in my own life—that sacrificial love. Would You give me a greater understanding of what love is? Help me to pray with love when I pray for others. Give me a greater love for You, so my life would reflect the fruits of righteousness and bring glory to You. Amen.

My prayer for: _____

_____

_____

_____

_____

_____

_____

_____

_____

What Would Happen?

2 Thessalonians 3:5
Read 2 Thessalonians 3

I have often wondered what would happen if believers all started praying differently. What if we forgot about focusing on the "little answerables" in people's lives—those everyday "make my life better" prayers we pray for people? I wonder what would happen if we all prayed more for the spiritual life of fellow believers than the physical life.

I don't know who said it, but several times I have heard a quote (once attributed to D.L. Moody and once to Billy Graham) that said of the U.S. church: "More than ninety-five percent of believers are of no consequence to the kingdom of God whatsoever, and in fact, may be a hindrance to it." Only God knows whether or not that is true. But if it is—or even if it is partially true—I bet it has something to do with how we pray for each other. We pray visible, surface stuff and seldom think to pray for the spiritual.

As he neared the end of his letter to the church at Thessalonica, Paul wrote: "We have confidence in the Lord that you are doing and will continue to do the things we command" (2 Thessalonians 3:4). But the interesting thing is that he didn't stop there. He didn't just preach at them or tell them how they should live and say, "Suck it up and do it!" He then went on to pray for them:

May the Lord direct your hearts into God's love and

Christ's perseverance. (2 Thessalonians 3:5)

As he did in his prayer for the Ephesian believers (Ephesians 3:16-19), Paul recognized that it was going to take a huge dose of the love of Christ infusing these believers for them to stay the course. It would require perseverance, the same kind of perseverance that kept Christ on course as He lived His life knowing what lay ahead of Him—the cross.

Many pastors put great prayer and effort into developing their sermons—into teaching their people. But come Monday morning, they are on to the next one. I wonder how much prayer goes into seeing that the application of their messages sinks into their people. I wonder if that isn't why Bill's (the pastor in the introduction to this devotional) situation is not unusual. Believers do not grow as they should because no one is praying for their spiritual health and growth.

What would happen if we all started praying for Christ's love and perseverance to permeate us and our fellow believers?

Prayer

Father, forgive me for focusing so many of my prayers on day-to-day comfort for people and so little on what really matters. I pray for _____ right now. Lord, would You fill him (or her) with a deeper sense of Your love for him? Let Your love fill _____ and pour out of him into the lives of others. Jesus, You persevered to the end. You kept going even knowing the cross was before You. Give _____ that same perseverance. Enable him to continue strong in the faith, despite all the circumstances that are weighing on him. Give _____ a "big picture" vision that will cause him to endure to the end. I pray this in Jesus' name, Amen.

My prayer for: _____

_____

_____

_____

_____

_____

_____

_____

_____

_____

_____

Wrestling in Prayer

Colossians 4:12
Read Colossians 4

When I was in fourth grade, I won second place in the elementary school (Watertown, NY) city wrestling championship (57-lb. weight class)! The championship bout was truly amazing. It came after we each had wrestled four bouts. We were tired but the adrenalin was pumping. We wrestled to a tie in regulation. After two overtimes we were still tied. I remember we were so dead that we literally just held on to each other for the entire last overtime. The winner was then determined by weight—whichever wrestler weighed less would win. I weighed 57 lbs. and he came in at 56!

I gave up wrestling in the seventh grade (I was 87 lbs. by then). For me, the effort and struggle of wrestling no longer matched my love for the sport.

Wrestling is hard work. It uses every bit of your strength, energy, stamina, and mental abilities (you have to strategize what the opponent's next move is). The apostle Paul talked about wrestling in prayer. He reminded the believers in Colosse that a friend—Epaphras—was wrestling in prayer for them:

> **Epaphras, who is one of you and a servant of Christ Jesus, sends greetings. He is always wrestling in prayer for you, that you may stand firm in all the will of God,**

mature and fully assured. (Colossians 4:12)

Have you ever wrestled in prayer for someone? I wonder what that would involve? Passion? Energy? Perseverance? Spiritual warfare that goes after the enemy? Epaphras was not wrestling over a physical, tangible need, but over a spiritual one. He was praying that the Colossians would stand firm in doing all the will of God. He didn't want wavering in their lives. "Lord, mature them. Give them full assurance of who they belong to."

Is there someone you know who needs a prayer like that? Someone who needs you to wrestle in prayer on his or her behalf? Ask God for the ability to wrestle for him or her.

Prayer

Lord Jesus, I lift up _____ to You. She (or he) needs a deeper awareness of who she is in Christ. Bring to her mind all she learned of You in the times she was walking closely with You. Don't let the enemy steal what You have put within her. Lord, give me the strength, energy, passion, and discernment I need to truly wrestle in prayer for her. Amen.

My prayer for: _____

_____

_____

_____

_____

Part 3

PRAYER AND THE MINISTRY OF THE GOSPEL

Pray for Me

Colossians 4:2-4
Read Colossians 4:2-6

A half dozen times in his epistles, Paul asked believers to pray for him. What is interesting to me, however, is what Paul asked them to pray for. There were no outward, tangible, personal needs mentioned. Instead, every request was that a spiritual dynamic or quality would manifest itself in his life.

When I compare the things I ask people to pray for me with Paul's requests, I am a little embarrassed. I am usually asking people to storm the gates of heaven for things to be fixed in my situations. While that certainly is not wrong, I wonder if I don't need to balance it. Perhaps I should be asking for prayer more for those kingdom-building things like Paul.

In Colossians, Paul requested:

> **Devote yourselves to prayer, being watchful and thankful. And pray for us, too, that God may open a door for our message, so that we may proclaim the mystery of Christ, for which I am in chains. Pray that I may proclaim it clearly, as I should. (Colossians 4:2-4)**

Paul wanted to be effective for the kingdom, even while he was in prison. If ever someone had a right to think *I need help right now. Get me out of this.* It was Paul. But instead, he wanted prayer that he would still have the ability to focus on kingdom work—*while in prison.* Pray for an opening to proclaim Christ, he requested. Pray for clarity. Interesting prayer, since Paul probably only saw guards and his jailers for short periods of time. He wanted to make the most of every opportunity.

Do we think to ask for prayer for those things? I need to do that more. Pray that I would be conscious of reaching out to people around me. I don't naturally think to do it. I need supernatural help! We all do.

Prayer

Lord Jesus, I don't instinctively reach out to people around me. I need Your enablement to do so. Holy Spirit, make me conscious of those I come in contact with who need a word of encouragement or truth. Nudge me strongly when there is someone in my day that You want me to share with. Fill me with Your heart for those around me. Then give me clarity to share something of lasting value in those quick moments I have. Lord, give me a hunger to be more devoted to prayer, which will in turn help me to keep my eyes open to Your opportunities. In Jesus' name I pray, Amen.

My prayer for: _____

_____

_____

_____

_____

_____

_____

_____

_____

Praying for the Lost

1 Timothy 2:1-4

Read Romans 10:1, Ephesians 6:19, and 1 Timothy 2:1-4

I have a close friend who believes that we do not need to pray for the lost. His reasoning is that nowhere in Scripture does it say that we are to pray for the lost. There are commands to pray for a few things—the peace of Jerusalem, laborers for the harvest, pray for your enemy—but nowhere does it command us to pray for the lost.

I have to gently disagree with my friend, but I can understand a little of his thinking. Nowhere is there a direct command, "pray for the lost," but we pray for a lot of things where there is not a direct command to do so. There are, however, some very clear evidences that Paul prayed for the lost.

While Paul was considered a missionary to the Gentiles, he had a burden for his own people who failed to recognize Jesus as the Christ, their Messiah.

Brothers, my heart's desire and prayer to God for the Israelites is that they may be saved. (Romans 10:1)

I don't think this "heart's desire and prayer" was just a passing fancy. He wasn't using the word *prayer* as we often do—"I pray that doesn't happen," meaning we are not really praying about this, but we hope something doesn't happen. Paul *was praying* for his people!

In another passage, Paul asked believers to pray for enablement and empowerment for him in his ministry of declaring the gospel.

> **Pray also for me, that whenever I open my mouth, words may be given me so that I will fearlessly make known the mystery of the gospel. (Ephesians 6:19)**

Certainly not a "pray for the lost" challenge, but clearly in that general arena.

Paul brought up prayer for the lost one more time—this one a little more direct:

> **I urge, then, first of all, that requests, prayers, intercession and thanksgiving be made for everyone—for kings and all those in authority, that we may live peaceful and quiet lives in all godliness and holiness. This is good, and pleases God our Savior, who wants all men to be saved and to come to a knowledge of the truth. (1 Timothy 2:1-4)**

The idea here is that we pray for certain things so people are more likely to come to a knowledge of the truth. Pray for national leaders—for peace and prosperity—so they will govern in a way that will allow people to live normal lives. This, indicated Paul, will bring people to a knowledge of the truth.

One of the interesting things I see here is that in two of these passages (Ephesians and 1 Timothy), Paul is not directly praying for the lost. He is praying for outside conditions to be manipulated so the situation is ripe for people to come into the kingdom.

There is a principle here that may be what my friend was hinting at by his belief that we shouldn't pray for the lost. I am not a theologian, so I do not understand all the free-will versus sovereignty-of-God arguments between differing camps. But I understand that God has given men enough free will to choose whether or not they will follow Jesus Christ.

As we pray for the lost, I believe God is at work. He is revealing Himself; He is bringing people and situations across the paths of nonbelievers that might cause them to think more of eternal things. He is thwarting Satan's grip on them, and for a time, shining light into their hearts. But He will not force them to choose Him. He will not override their free will.

So as we pray for specific lost people, we need to remember this principle: Is what we are asking in line with what God would do in pursuit of this person? Or are our prayers attempting to manipulate the person's free will?

Prayer

Father, I lift up _____ to You right now. My heart's desire, Lord, is that he (or she) would come to saving faith in You. Lord, would You bring about circumstances in his life that get him thinking about his spiritual need? Stir up in him a longing for You. I pray that You would put dynamic, winsome believers in his path, people he likes and respects, whose personalities draw him. Give me words to speak into his life that would make him think. Allow him windows of opportunity where Your light will shine into his heart. Hold back the forces of darkness that seek to manipulate his thoughts. Bring him to the end of himself so he desires a Savior. Amen.

My prayer for: _____

_____

_____

_____

_____

_____

_____

_____

_____

_____

Warring in Prayer

2 Thessalonians 3:1-2

Read 2 Thessalonians 3:1-5

While we do not consciously think of this all the time, when we become believers, we are truly entering a war. The war between good and evil, between Satan's forces and God's. Satan is trying to thwart believers and put us on the sidelines—especially those who are working for the kingdom.

Satan hates to see prayer happen. He knows that when we pray, God is up to something. So he does everything he can to keep us from prayer. We need to learn to fight back. We need, as Ephesians 6 tells us, to put on the armor of God. Then we need to keep "praying for all the saints" (Ephesians 6:18).

Paul asked the believers in Thessalonica to war in prayer on his behalf:

> Finally, brothers, pray for us that the message of the Lord may spread rapidly and be honored, just as it was with you. And pray that we may be delivered from wicked and evil men, for not everyone has faith. (2 Thessalonians 3:1-2)

He asked them to focus on the rapid spreading of the gospel. But, he said, evil men (directed by Satan) try to stop it. He asked his fellow believers to come against those wicked men so the spread of the gospel could go forward.

As we pray for our pastors, leaders and friends who are working for the kingdom, we need to remember this request as well. Satan continually sends messengers to try to distract, thwart, and stop the work of God from happening in a church or ministry. We need to develop a habit of coming against those "evil men" that Satan manipulates to do his work.

Prayer

Father, I lift up my pastor to You right now. I know he is under attack. Protect Your shepherd, Lord. Send angels around him to keep Satan's evil men from distracting him. In the mighty name of Jesus, I come against anyone in my pastor's life who is doing the work of Satan to thwart, harm, or distract. I declare: You cannot hinder him any more, in Jesus' name! Lord Jesus, empower and enable my pastor to be effective for Your kingdom. Open doors so Your gospel can spread through his life and our church. In Jesus' name, Amen.

My prayer for: _____

_____

_____

_____

_____

_____

_____

_____

Declare It

Ephesians 6:19-20
Read Ephesians 6:10-20

I grew up in a denomination with a strong missions emphasis, where we had a tendency to put missionaries on a pedestal. They were the frontline guys, the ones who were really sacrificing for the faith. When a young person announced she felt called to missionary service (it meant overseas, of course), she was honored within her church.

While the emphasis and respect we gave to the person was good, it sometimes made him or her larger than life. Those individuals were the super-Christians. We forgot they were human, with human feelings, human struggles, human shortcomings.

Paul was a super-Christian in our minds as well. Yet in Ephesians 6 he asked for prayer to overcome what must have been a shortcoming. He struggled to speak clearly and fearlessly about the gospel. What? *Paul* struggled with words and shyness?

Paul's request was this:

> **Pray also for me, that whenever I open my mouth, words may be given me so that I will fearlessly make known the mystery of the gospel, for which I am an ambassador in chains. Pray that I may declare it fearlessly, as I should. (Ephesians 6:19-20)**

Think about that missionary you know, or that young person preparing for the mission field. What are his personality traits that might make missionary service a challenge? You understand that if a person struggles to share his faith in the home country, he won't automatically be able to in another culture. Only God can enable—and that will come through prayer.

So when you pray for that missionary (or friend) you know personally, remember those traits that need God's enablement to be overcome and used for His glory.

∽

Prayer

Father, I hold _____ and _____ before your throne and ask for Your enablement in their lives. _____ needs encouragement to stay the course. Give him signs that You are with him and that he is doing Your will. And in _____'s struggle with shyness, be her strong right arm! Give a fearlessness that can only come through Your Holy Spirit. Empower them both to reach out and build relationships. Especially lead them to those relationships that will bear lasting fruit, people coming into Your kingdom. I pray this in the mighty name of Jesus, Amen.

My prayer for: _____

_____

_____

_____

_____

_____

_____

_____

_____

_____

_____

_____

Praying for Those in Ministry

Romans 15:30-32
Read Romans 15:23-33

Interceding for those in ministry is something many believers are called to do. As we mature in the faith and in our prayer lives, God will often give us a burden for a particular person in ministry: a missionary who was sent out from our church or who came to our church to share; a pastor; perhaps a friend or relative who is called to full-time ministry.

As we grow in this area it is also not uncommon to be awakened in the night with that person on our mind, or to have that person pop into our minds at some time during the day. Often when this happens it is so we can pray for him or her. Something is happening in that person's life right then, or will happen soon, and God is nudging us to pray. Sometimes it is an intense sensation. We are driven to prayer and cannot stop until we feel a release in our spirits.

Romans 15:30-32 relates to this issue. It is not a prayer of Paul's, but a place where Paul asked the Roman believers to pray for him. Paul was not asking for weak, quick prayers. In fact he asked them to "struggle." Then, much like a modern missionary prayer letter, he gave them some specific things to pray for him:

> **I urge, you, brothers, by our Lord Jesus Christ and by the love of the Spirit, to join me in my struggle by praying to God for me. Pray that I may be rescued from the**

unbelievers in Judea and that my service in Jerusalem may be acceptable to the saints there, so that by God's will I may come to you with joy and together with you be refreshed. (Romans 15:30-32)

Paul asked them to pray for two things:

1. For safety and protection. "Pray that I may be rescued from unbelievers." If you read through the book of Acts you will see how difficult Paul had it. People were constantly trying to stop him, harm him, even kill him. (Jews who did not convert in cities where Paul ministered were constantly plotting to kill him.) Paul told the Corinthian believers that in his heart he "felt the sentence of death" (2 Corinthians 1:9). As we pray what God has placed on our hearts for those who minister, we need to remember that they are on the front lines fighting the battle against Satan. They need protection. They need to remain solid in the faith to stand firm.

In his famous warfare chapter in Ephesians 6, after listing all the weapons and armor we have as believers, Paul wrote, "*with this in mind*, be alert and always keep on praying for all the saints" (6:18, *emphasis added*). "With this in mind" refers to the fact that we are in a battle. We need to remember that and struggle in prayer for believers on the front lines.

2. That things would be smooth with the believers in Jerusalem. Satan often uses difficulties in relationships among believers—especially those who are working on the front lines to spread the gospel—to thwart effective ministry. Many a missionary has had to be reassigned or leave the ministry because of relationship difficulties with other missionaries or national church leaders. We need to remember to pray continually for good, solid, loving relationships between missionaries so that they can be effective for the kingdom.

Prayer

Lord Jesus, You have called _____ to minister for Your kingdom in _____. I know the evil one wants to hinder him (or her) from fulfilling that call. I ask right now that You would send angels round about him, to protect and shield him from Satan's attacks. I pray that You would give him open doors with unbelievers. I pray that they would be drawn to him, instead of desiring to stop him. I also pray that You would give him an unusual ability to get along with his missions team. I pray for strong relationships and friendships with his fellow workers. Help him to rise above those character traits that annoy him or others. Provide _____ with the ability to be a peacemaker. I pray these things in the mighty name of Jesus Christ. Amen.

My prayer for: _____

Through Your Prayers

Philippians 1:19, 2 Corinthians 1:10-11

Read 2 Corinthians 1:8-11 and Philippians 1:19-26

This past year has easily been the most difficult year of ministry for my wife and myself. (We are in full-time, raise-your-own-support prayer ministry.) There has been so much attack that we have seriously considered whether or not we were in God's will. I mean, His blessing should be with us if we are doing His will, right?

When I became the head of the Church Prayer Leaders Network, Joseph Winger, the outgoing director, told me that the previous two years (the time he led the CPLN) were among the most rewarding years of his ministry, but they were also the toughest. He warned me that the attack would be relentless. It has been. When we are doing God's kingdom work, Satan tries to stop it. We need continual prayer.

In two of his letters, Paul pleaded for prayer:

I know that through your prayers and the help given by the Spirit of Jesus Christ, what has happened to me will turn out for my deliverance. (Philippians 1:19)

He has delivered us from such a deadly peril, and he will deliver us. On him we have set our hope that he will continue to deliver us, as you help us by your prayers. Then many will give thanks on our behalf for the gra-

cious favor granted us in answer to the prayers of many. (2 Corinthians 1:10-11)

Prayer is a mystery. We know God is sovereign and in control, yet we are told to pray. Why? Does God need our prayers? Apparently, for whatever reason, God has restricted Himself with the stipulation that He will use humans to help further His kingdom through prayer. He responds to prayer. But . . . He also initiates the prayer. It is an endless cycle. God puts in your heart the need to pray. You pray. God responds.

Paul needed the prayers of the Corinthian church. He needed the prayers of the Philippian believers. And there are people in ministry who desperately need your prayers. If you are in ministry, you need the prayers of other believers.

When you feel a nudge or tug to pray for someone, do it! God is initiating. He needs you to pray. If you are going through tough times or a struggle, ask God to move people around you to pray.

Prayer

Father God, thank You that You have ordained that we could have a part in Your kingdom work through prayer. Thank You for that awesome privilege. Please use me to further Your kingdom. Nudge me, prod me, compel me to pray for specific people who need Your hand of protection or guidance. Lord Jesus, I lift up _____ to You now. You have laid her (or him) on my heart. Show me what to pray for her. (pause) She seems to be going through the wringer right now. Send angels around her and her family to protect them. Give them the encouragement and strength they need to endure this battle. Bring relief to their situation. Show Yourself mighty in their midst! In Jesus' name, Amen.

My prayer for: _____

_____

_____

_____

_____

_____

_____

_____

_____

Part 4

PRAYING FOR OTHER BELIEVERS

A Healthy Heart

1 Thessalonians 3:12-13
Read 1 Thessalonians 3

A healthy heart is crucial to a healthy body. Because blood pumping through our veins is so important, having a defective pump can be life threatening. In the spiritual life, we need a healthy heart as well. But our spiritual heart does not pump blood—it pumps love. Love is crucial for growing a healthy believer—love for God and love for those around us.

If we do not love God, our service for Him will be lacking. If we serve at all, it will be out of duty or fear. We will not care that our sinful lives grieve a holy God. If we do not love others, we will not

73

care enough to share the good news of Christ with them; we will not sacrifice for others. We will not be concerned that our actions confuse or hurt others.

Paul prayed for strong hearts for the Thessalonian believers—hearts that flowed with love.

> **May the Lord make your love increase and overflow for each other and for everyone else, just as ours does for you. May he strengthen your hearts so that you will be blameless and holy in the presence of our God and Father when our Lord Jesus comes with all his holy ones. (1 Thessalonians 3:12-13)**

Paul specifically asked Jesus Christ to increase the believers' love for each other. That increase of love would bring a great will to live lives pleasing to God. Sometimes we get frustrated with fellow believers when they do not live up to our spiritual expectations. We also get frustrated with ourselves and our failings. Maybe we just need stronger hearts. Maybe if we started praying for more love—for an overflow of love—the rest would take care of itself.

Prayer

Father, I pray that _____ would overflow with Your love. Pour out the love of Jesus on him (or her). Please let him sense Your love for him. Then cause that knowledge of Your love to grow love within _____. May love for others ooze out of him. Father God, strengthen _____'s heart so that he can overcome the evil one and live a pure and

blameless life before You. May _____ be a model
follower of Yours so others can emulate his life. Amen.

My prayer for: _____

_____

_____

_____

_____

_____

_____

_____

_____

_____

Supernatural Unity

Romans 15:5-6
Read Romans 15:1-7

Unity is one of the most difficult things to maintain in the life of a church and between individual believers. As individuals we have differing opinions on everything. And it is common for people to think that anyone who does not see things exactly as they do is wrong.

Satan uses this to his advantage in churches. He drives little wedges between people. He uses style of music, subtleties in theology, decorating tastes, how we discipline our children ... you name it, he uses it to bring disunity!

The church at Rome was experiencing disunity. The first verses of chapter 15 hint at this problem. After mentioning it, Paul then prayed:

> May the God who gives endurance and encouragement give you a spirit of unity among yourselves as you follow Christ Jesus, so that with all your heart and mouth you may glorify the God and Father of our Lord Jesus Christ. (Romans 15:5-6)

Unity was important to Paul—and to God. Why? What does unity among believers do?

Remember Jesus' prayer in John 17? "I pray also for those

who will believe in me through their message, that all of them may be one, Father, just as you are in me and I am in you. May they also be in us so that the world may believe that you have sent me" (vv. 20-21).

While Jesus was talking to all believers, the universal Church, I think we can bring it down to the local church level as well. Something happens in the heavenly realm when the church is unified. Jesus said that people will recognize who He is and will believe. When a church is in unity, evangelism will happen easily! No wonder Satan does everything he can to keep us from having unity! He knew that Jesus Christ would receive glory if unity occurred among the Roman believers. People would be drawn to Him when they saw the unity of the Roman believers. They will be drawn to Him through your church as well—if there is unity.

Prayer

Lord Jesus, You said that when You were lifted up, You would draw all men to Yourself. You also prayed for unity so that people would know who You are and be drawn to You. Lord, do a mighty work in our church to bring unity. God who gives endurance and encouragement, would You give me the perseverance and strength I need to work through the differences I have with other believers in my church and community, to show grace to others who have different opinions, tastes, and ideas than I do? Help me to see that I don't have to have the same opinions as everyone else in order to be in unity. We can be different and still be unified in You! Make me a champion for unity in my church, so You would be glorified. Amen.

My prayer for: _____

_____

_____

_____

_____

_____

_____

_____

_____

_____

Every Good Thing We Have in Christ

Philemon 6
Read Philemon 1-7

I grew up in the church. As a kid, I remember having times in services—usually Sunday nights—where we had "testimony time." The pastor would ask if those assembled had anything to share about what God was doing in their lives. People would pop up and share something they wanted to thank God for. A physical healing, protection, a chance to share the gospel with a friend were all fodder for testimony time. I even remember some services where that was all we did—the pastor never got to preach because people were sharing so much.

I don't know why, but somewhere along the line churches stopped doing that. Maybe it's due to most churches today not having a Sunday night service, and this "out of control" free-for-all wasn't deemed appropriate for the Sunday morning service. We lost something, however. Those sessions were exciting. What would we hear to praise God for? We heard of God's faithfulness. His healing power. His overwhelming love. The way He worked in people's lives to bring them to a decision. How the Holy Spirit illuminated light into dark hearts. His power to solve tremendous problems.

In the book of Philemon, Paul was writing a letter to an old friend—a solid believer. The bulk of the one-chapter book is Paul asking Philemon to receive back into his household a runaway slave named Onesimus. It seemed that Onesimus had come into contact with Paul and had become a believer. Paul was asking his former owner to forgive Onesimus and receive him back as a brother.

Paul started the letter by encouraging Philemon. Paul saw his great love for the saints, how Philemon cared for them and was concerned about them. He wanted that same love and concern for this new brother—even though Onesimus had wronged Philemon. In the midst of all this, Paul shared that he was praying something for Philemon. Something curious, given the circumstances:

> **I pray that you may be active in sharing your faith, so that you will have a full understanding of every good thing we have in Christ. (Philemon 6)**

What in the world was the connection between being active in sharing his faith (remember the context of this passage is sharing faith with believers—not witnessing to unbelievers) and Philemon understanding all he had in Christ? I think the connection is exactly what was happening in those old testimony meetings.

When we share with others what Christ is doing in our lives (or when we hear others share the same with us) three things happen:

1. Our faith grows. We gain a deeper desire to love and serve the One who is doing all these powerful things. We gain more faith and experience more of Jesus Christ's reality. We also keep our eyes open for things to share.

2. The more we share or hear others share, the more we learn about God's attributes. We come to know Him as our Provider, our Rock, our Comforter, our Peace-Giver, our Protector, our Strong Tower, our Deliverer. We learn exactly what Paul wanted Philemon to learn—what he had in Christ.

3. When we regularly share, thus giving glory to Jesus Christ, I believe that God works overtime in our lives. He wants to give us more to share, so we give more glory and fame to His Son. So it is a cycle. See God work; learn something about God; share it; see God work more; understand more of God's nature.

Prayer

Father, please work mightily in _____'s situation. Reveal more of Your nature and character to her (or him). Father, I pray that _____ would understand all she has in Jesus Christ: the depth of His love; the comfort, power, and enablement of Your Holy Spirit. Let Your Spirit bubble up in her so it would overflow into others. I pray this in Jesus' name, Amen.

My prayer for: _____

_____

_____

_____

_____

_____

_____

_____

_____

_____

The Power of Mentoring

Have you ever noticed that with some believers you just know that they are growing in their faith, but with others, you do not see signs that their walk with God is going anywhere? What makes the difference?

Certainly some do not have a strong desire to grow. They have made some commitment to Christ, but it does not go deep enough to radically shape the way they live. But many believers simply have not had any real encouragement to grow. No one has ever come alongside them to mentor or disciple them. I bet most believers who are active in their faith have at points in their lives had people encouraging them and challenging them in their walk with Jesus. Someone modeled what a vibrant faith looks like for them.

Paul did that for his converts. People up and down Asia Minor who were in the churches planted by Paul grew because of Paul's personal interest in them. Paul prayed regularly for them. And he prayed that God might grant him a way to touch their lives personally again.

Night and day we pray most earnestly that we may see you again and supply what is lacking in your faith. Now may our God and Father himself and our Lord Jesus clear the way for us to come to you. (1 Thessalonians 3:10-11)

What about you? Are you actively praying for ways to mentor a fellow believer? No matter where you are in your faith's journey, no matter what is lacking in your knowledge of Jesus Christ, someone could use your encouragement. Someone is not as far along as you! Why not begin to pray for that person? Then look for ways to encourage, sharpen, and challenge him or her in the faith. Become a mentor like Paul.

Prayer

Father, I lift up _____ to You right now. I know he (or she) has a heart for You, but lacks a drive or desire to go deeper. I pray that You would give him a greater hunger and passion to know You. Draw him to Yourself, O Lord. Show me ways that I might be an encouragement to him in his walk with You. I am willing, if You would open the door, for me to mentor _____. Just show me the action I should take. Amen.

My prayer for: _____

_____

_____

_____

_____

_____

_____

_____

Stay Focused

2 Thessalonians 2:16-17
Read 2 Thessalonians 2

I am old enough to remember various periods where the church seemed unusually focused on end-time prophecy. The early seventies and the late eighties are two such periods. Multiple books filled with end-time predictions became best sellers. Traveling evangelists who preached on end-time scenarios were popular. Everyone was predicting who the Antichrist was: Yassar Arafat, Saddam Hussein. Many were fixated on the need to know these things.

It is important to remember that Jesus Christ is returning—the "second coming," we call it. But rather than be fixated on the "what and how," we need to let our longing for the second coming drive us to kingdom work. The church of the late 1700s and then the late 1800s both had seasons where the second coming was in the forefront of believers' minds. It drove believers to sacrifice to build Christ's kingdom on earth as it was in heaven. Missionary movements flourished; the church built hospitals and took care of the poor in unprecedented ways. All this was driven by a desire to bring back the King! When that last tribe heard the gospel, Jesus was coming back. So the cry was, "Let's get missionaries out there to tell the tribes!"

The Thessalonian believers of Paul's day seemed to be fixated a little with the second coming. Paul challenged them to remember that it had not occurred yet. They needed to keep pressing forward, to keep standing firm in their faith. He exhorted them not to get sidetracked by the rumors they heard. Then he prayed for them:

May our Lord Jesus Christ himself and God our Father, who loved us and by his grace gave us eternal encouragement and good hope, encourage your hearts and strengthen you in every good deed and word. (2 Thessalonians 2:16-17)

What did Paul pray for? Encouragement and strength to keep doing good deeds and to continue speaking the truth. He did not want them to get sidetracked by thoughts that the end was near, but rather, to keep working for the kingdom.

Do you know any fellow believers who get fixated and sidetracked on spiritual issues such as the second coming. They get in a blather over theological differences and trying to prove their position is correct. Perhaps they need to be prayed for like Paul prayed for the Thessalonian church.

Prayer

Father, I know how easy it is to get sidetracked into unimportant issues. I think _____ is struggling with that right now. You love her (or him) and have a purpose for her. I pray that You would encourage her heart to keep moving forward with Your purposes. Speak to _____, and reveal Your heart to her. Give her strength to move past that issue that seems to be keeping her from the spiritual things that really matter. Use

_____ to spread good deeds and speak truth for
Your kingdom's sake. I pray this in Jesus' name, Amen.

My prayer for: _____

_____

_____

_____

_____

_____

_____

_____

_____

_____

Thanking God for Those Who Serve

1 Thessalonians 1:2-3
Read 1 Thessalonians 1

Have you ever thought about how blessed you are by fellow believers in your life? Think of your family if they are Christians. Consider your brothers and sisters in the faith who impact you. That small group leader or Sunday school teacher who continually works to grow spiritual truth in your life. The children's worker who tirelessly encourages your kids each week. That elder at church who always makes it a point to come over and chat with you whenever he sees you. Your pastor. People who pray for you and your family.

Have you ever thought of thanking God for them? Thanking God for their faith, love, and dedication to Him?

That's exactly what Paul was doing with his prayer in 1 Thessalonians 1:2-3. While these were believers *he* was discipling, not ones who were discipling him, the principle is the same. He brought fellow believers before the throne and simply thanked God for them.

We always thank God for all of you, mentioning you in our prayers. We continually remember before our God

and Father your work produced by faith, your labor
prompted by love, and your endurance inspired by hope
in our Lord Jesus Christ. (1 Thessalonians 1:2-3)

When we study this prayer, we see something deeper than just
Paul's thankful heart expressed in prayer. While Paul *was* thanking
God for them, more seems to be implied. He was also continuing
to ask God to develop these wonderful qualities in them. He re-
membered their labor for the kingdom, which he says was the result
of their powerful faith. "Faith without works," James reminds us,
"is dead!" (See James 2:26, KJV). "Lord, thanks for giving them
faith," Paul was saying, "but keep increasing it. Nurture it, Lord
Jesus. Cause them to be energized by laboring for You."

The next time you go to prayer, spend some time remembering to
the Lord believers who touch your life. Thank Him for what He has
done in them to bless you. Then ask for those qualities to mature and
grow in them as well. As an ongoing prayer pattern, select one or a
few to regularly uphold before the Father in humble thanks.

Prayer

Lord Jesus, I thank You for what You are doing in _____'s
life. I am deeply blessed by _____ (service for the
kingdom that touches you) _____. Enable and empower him
(or her) to minister effectively. Do not let him get discouraged in the
trenches of ministry, but fill him with joy in serving You! Amen.

My prayer for: _____

Praying for Other Believers

_____

_____

_____

_____

_____

_____

_____

_____

Thanking God for Others

Colossians 1:3-4
Read Colossians 1:1-8

One of the areas of my life that I struggle to improve in is relationships. I get in my own little world with my work and ministry and often do not take the time to develop friendships. But recently, during a time of intense spiritual attack and overwhelming pressure in our ministry, I noticed something.

It was the dedication of friends and fellow believers surrounding the putting on of our national prayer conference, Empowered. We watched our Columbia, SC, friends, Jim, Susan, H.L., Janie, and Marian provide incredible sacrifice to make this conference a success. They gave hours of time, sweat, prayer, and physical labor to bring about Empowered. I found myself thanking God for them time and time again through the process—and especially during the week of the event.

It was their faith in Jesus, their love for us, and their desire to see their church grow into a strong praying church that drove them to sacrifice. I need to get better at recognizing that dedication in fellow believers, and thanking God for it.

Paul did that. In his letter to the church at Colosse, he expressed his gratitude for these believers, by sharing what he was telling God about them:

We always thank God, the Father of our Lord Jesus

Christ, when we pray for you, because we have heard of your faith in Christ Jesus and of the love you have for all the saints. (Colossians 1:3-4)

We need each other in the body of Christ. And we need to bless others who demonstrate the love and passion of Jesus in their lives. We also need to thank God continually for people who live out their faith. What believers stand out in your life as those who are modeling their faith well? Thank God for them!

Prayer

Father, I thank You for _____ and _____, who have given of themselves so sacrificially. Thank You for the gifts You gave to them. Thank You for the love they have for You and Your church that drove them to sacrifice. Thank You for their sweet spirits and servant's hearts that could only come through Your Holy Spirit's enablement. I bless You, Father, for bringing these precious saints into my life to model Your love for me. Father, I pray that You would shower them with a special blessing this week to let them know of Your pleasure. In Jesus' name, Amen.

My prayer for: _____

_____

_____

_____

_____

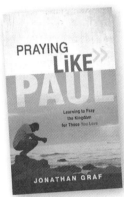
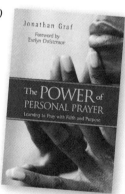